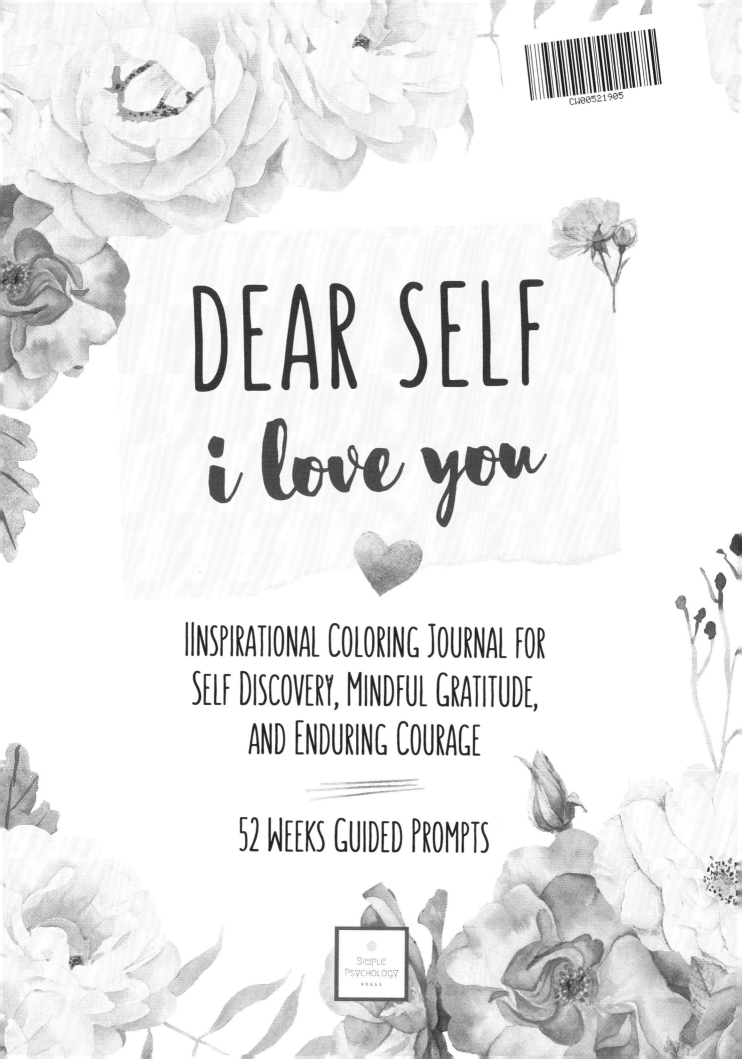

# DEAR SELF
## *i love you*

IInspirational Coloring Journal for
Self Discovery, Mindful Gratitude,
and Enduring Courage

52 Weeks Guided Prompts

SIMPLE
PSYCHOLOGY
PRESS

# Before you begin...

- *prepare a warm drink, collect your coloring materials, and find a shaded spot outside where you can sit back and be close to nature, if this is possible.*

- *sharpen your coloring pencils if you have them, and if you are using heavy markers, use the color test page (p.107) to check for bleed through.*

- *relax and have fun... enjoy making this book as personal as possible by putting your own unique creativity into it.*

- *remember to visit this journal every day to meditate on the guided prompts for the week.*

**ISBN-13: 979-8643413288**

We are so glad you have our book!
For queries email us at: simplepsychologypress@gmail.com

*Dwell on the beauty of life. Watch the stars, and see yourself running with them.*

MARCUS AURELIUS

THIS JOURNAL BELONGS TO

_____

_____

_____

# 3 New Things I Enjoyed Doing Today

DATE:

- _____
- _____
- _____

DATE:

- _____
- _____
- _____

DATE:

- _____
- _____
- _____

DATE:

- _____
- _____
- _____

DATE:

- _____
- _____
- _____

DATE:

- _____
- _____
- _____

DATE:

- _____
- _____
- _____

**TODAY**

IS THE START OF
SOMETHING NEW.

# 3 Thoughts That Makes Me Happy

DATE:
- _____
- _____
- _____

DATE:
- _____
- _____
- _____

DATE:
- _____
- _____
- _____

DATE:
- _____
- _____
- _____

DATE:
- _____
- _____
- _____

DATE:
- _____
- _____
- _____

DATE:
- _____
- _____
- _____

# 3 Kind Ways to Treat Myself Today

DATE:
- _____
- _____
- _____

DATE:
- _____
- _____
- _____

DATE:
- _____
- _____
- _____

DATE:
- _____
- _____
- _____

DATE:
- _____
- _____
- _____

DATE:
- _____
- _____
- _____

DATE:
- _____
- _____
- _____

I am gentle
with myself.
I am doing the best
I can.

# 3 Things That Completes My Day

DATE:
- _____
- _____
- _____

DATE:
- _____
- _____
- _____

DATE:
- _____
- _____
- _____

DATE:
- _____
- _____
- _____

DATE:
- _____
- _____
- _____

DATE:
- _____
- _____
- _____

DATE:
- _____
- _____
- _____

# 3 Thoughts That Puts Me In A Good Mood

DATE:

- _____
- _____
- _____

DATE:

- _____
- _____
- _____

DATE:

- _____
- _____
- _____

DATE:

- _____
- _____
- _____

DATE:

- _____
- _____
- _____

DATE:

- _____
- _____
- _____

DATE:

- _____
- _____
- _____

"The most important decision
you will ever make
is to be in a good mood."

Voltaire

# 3 Moments That Brings Me Happiness

DATE:

- _____
- _____
- _____

DATE:

- _____
- _____
- _____

DATE:

- _____
- _____
- _____

DATE:

- _____
- _____
- _____

DATE:

- _____
- _____
- _____

DATE:

- _____
- _____
- _____

DATE:

- _____
- _____
- _____

# 3 Things That Made Me Feel Braver Today

**DATE:**
- _____
- _____
- _____

**DATE:**
- _____
- _____
- _____

**DATE:**
- _____
- _____
- _____

**DATE:**
- _____
- _____
- _____

**DATE:**
- _____
- _____
- _____

**DATE:**
- _____
- _____
- _____

**DATE:**
- _____
- _____
- _____

# 3 Reasons Why I Believe in Myself

DATE:
- _____
- _____
- _____

DATE:
- _____
- _____
- _____

DATE:
- _____
- _____
- _____

DATE:
- _____
- _____
- _____

DATE:
- _____
- _____
- _____

DATE:
- _____
- _____
- _____

DATE:
- _____
- _____
- _____

# i can be the happiest version of me

# 3 Positively Powerful Words to Describe Me

DATE:
- _____
- _____
- _____

DATE:
- _____
- _____
- _____

DATE:
- _____
- _____
- _____

DATE:
- _____
- _____
- _____

DATE:
- _____
- _____
- _____

DATE:
- _____
- _____
- _____

DATE:
- _____
- _____
- _____

# self love is my super power

# 3 Mistakes That Helped Me Grow & Learn

DATE:
- _____
- _____
- _____

DATE:
- _____
- _____
- _____

DATE:
- _____
- _____
- _____

DATE:
- _____
- _____
- _____

DATE:
- _____
- _____
- _____

DATE:
- _____
- _____
- _____

DATE:
- _____
- _____
- _____

# 3 Brave Ways to Help Me Keep Moving

**DATE:**
- _____
- _____
- _____

**DATE:**
- _____
- _____
- _____

**DATE:**
- _____
- _____
- _____

**DATE:**
- _____
- _____
- _____

**DATE:**
- _____
- _____
- _____

**DATE:**
- _____
- _____
- _____

**DATE:**
- _____
- _____
- _____

"You must tell yourself,
no matter how hard it is
or how hard it gets,
I'm going to make it."

Les Brown

# 3 Quick Ways I Can Restore My Balance

**DATE:**
- _____
- _____
- _____

**DATE:**
- _____
- _____
- _____

**DATE:**
- _____
- _____
- _____

**DATE:**
- _____
- _____
- _____

**DATE:**
- _____
- _____
- _____

**DATE:**
- _____
- _____
- _____

**DATE:**
- _____
- _____
- _____

breathe

# 3 Past Hurts I Am Finally Letting Go Of

DATE:

- _____
- _____
- _____

DATE:

- _____
- _____
- _____

DATE:

- _____
- _____
- _____

DATE:

- _____
- _____
- _____

DATE:

- _____
- _____
- _____

DATE:

- _____
- _____
- _____

DATE:

- _____
- _____
- _____

"Breathe.
Let go.
And remind
yourself that
this very
moment is
the only one
you know
you have
for sure."

Oprah Winfrey

# 3 Things That Makes Me Feel Stronger

DATE:
- _____
- _____
- _____

DATE:
- _____
- _____
- _____

DATE:
- _____
- _____
- _____

DATE:
- _____
- _____
- _____

DATE:
- _____
- _____
- _____

DATE:
- _____
- _____
- _____

DATE:
- _____
- _____
- _____

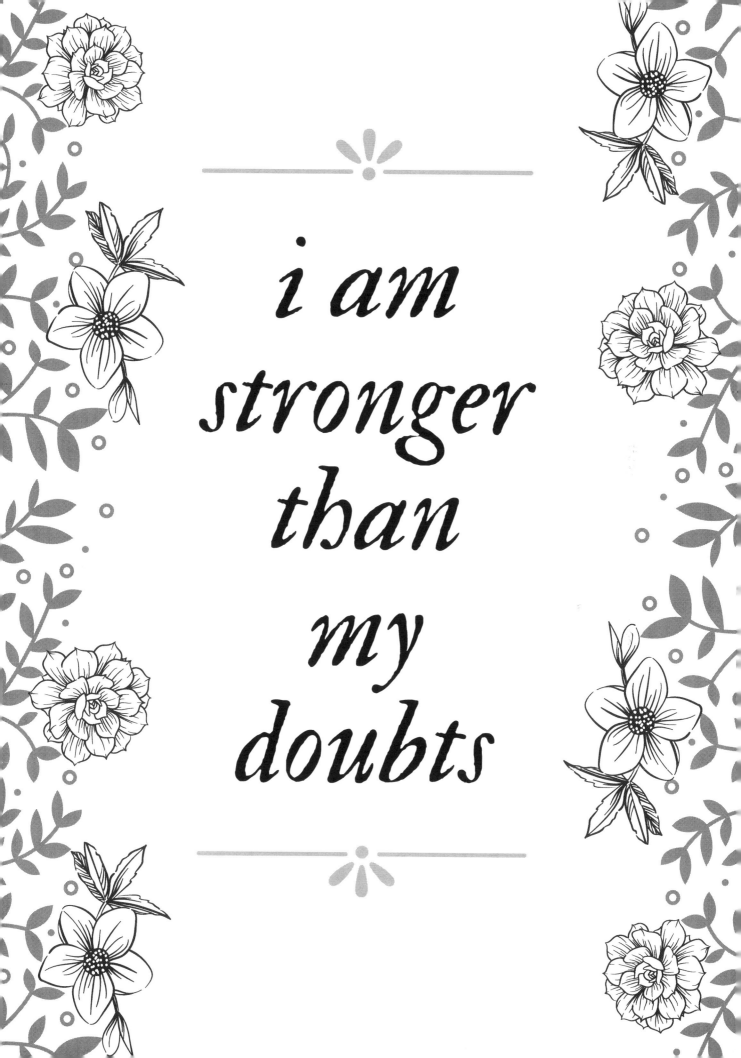

i am
stronger
than
my
doubts

# 3 Reasons To Be Proud Of Today

**DATE:**
- _____
- _____
- _____

**DATE:**
- _____
- _____
- _____

**DATE:**
- _____
- _____
- _____

**DATE:**
- _____
- _____
- _____

**DATE:**
- _____
- _____
- _____

**DATE:**
- _____
- _____
- _____

**DATE:**
- _____
- _____
- _____

The best view
comes after
the hardest
climb.

# 3 Wise Words To Describe My Life So Far

DATE:
- _____
- _____
- _____

DATE:
- _____
- _____
- _____

DATE:
- _____
- _____
- _____

DATE:
- _____
- _____
- _____

DATE:
- _____
- _____
- _____

DATE:
- _____
- _____
- _____

DATE:
- _____
- _____
- _____

I lost
my way
all the way
to you
and in you
I found
all the way
back to me.

Atticus

# 3 Thoughts That Gives Me Inner Strength

**DATE:**
- _____
- _____
- _____

**DATE:**
- _____
- _____
- _____

**DATE:**
- _____
- _____
- _____

**DATE:**
- _____
- _____
- _____

**DATE:**
- _____
- _____
- _____

**DATE:**
- _____
- _____
- _____

**DATE:**
- _____
- _____
- _____

"For what it's worth, it's
never too late to be
whoever you want to be.

I hope you live a life
you're proud of...
and if you find that
you're not, I hope you
have the strength to
start over."

F. Scott Fitzgerald

# 3 People I Am Thankful For Today

**DATE:**
- _____
- _____
- _____

**DATE:**
- _____
- _____
- _____

**DATE:**
- _____
- _____
- _____

**DATE:**
- _____
- _____
- _____

**DATE:**
- _____
- _____
- _____

**DATE:**
- _____
- _____
- _____

**DATE:**
- _____
- _____
- _____

There is always something to be thankful for.

# 3 Things I Love About Myself

DATE:

- _____
- _____
- _____

DATE:

- _____
- _____
- _____

DATE:

- _____
- _____
- _____

DATE:

- _____
- _____
- _____

DATE:

- _____
- _____
- _____

DATE:

- _____
- _____
- _____

DATE:

- _____
- _____
- _____

"Love
yourself
first and
everything
falls into
line."

Lucille Ball

# 3 Challenges I Overcame Today

DATE:
- _____
- _____
- _____

DATE:
- _____
- _____
- _____

DATE:
- _____
- _____
- _____

DATE:
- _____
- _____
- _____

DATE:
- _____
- _____
- _____

DATE:
- _____
- _____
- _____

DATE:
- _____
- _____
- _____

i will
fly
above
the
storm

# 3 Promises to Myself That Gives Me Courage

**DATE:**
- _____
- _____
- _____

**DATE:**
- _____
- _____
- _____

**DATE:**
- _____
- _____
- _____

**DATE:**
- _____
- _____
- _____

**DATE:**
- _____
- _____
- _____

**DATE:**
- _____
- _____
- _____

**DATE:**
- _____
- _____
- _____

*storms*

don't last forever

# 3 Words that Can Instantly Give Me Comfort

**DATE:**
- _____
- _____
- _____

**DATE:**
- _____
- _____
- _____

**DATE:**
- _____
- _____
- _____

**DATE:**
- _____
- _____
- _____

**DATE:**
- _____
- _____
- _____

**DATE:**
- _____
- _____
- _____

**DATE:**
- _____
- _____
- _____

# 3 Places That Helps Me Feel Calm & Relax

DATE:
- _____
- _____
- _____

DATE:
- _____
- _____
- _____

DATE:
- _____
- _____
- _____

DATE:
- _____
- _____
- _____

DATE:
- _____
- _____
- _____

DATE:
- _____
- _____
- _____

DATE:
- _____
- _____
- _____

WHEREVER LIFE
PLANTS ME

*I will bloom
with Grace*

# 3 Things That Kept Me Going Today

DATE:

- _____
- _____
- _____

DATE:

- _____
- _____
- _____

DATE:

- _____
- _____
- _____

DATE:

- _____
- _____
- _____

DATE:

- _____
- _____
- _____

DATE:

- _____
- _____
- _____

DATE:

- _____
- _____
- _____

"Our greatest glory
is not in never
failing, but in rising
every time we fall."

Confucius

# 3 New Things I Am Most Excited To Try

DATE:
- _____
- _____
- _____

DATE:
- _____
- _____
- _____

DATE:
- _____
- _____
- _____

DATE:
- _____
- _____
- _____

DATE:
- _____
- _____
- _____

DATE:
- _____
- _____
- _____

DATE:
- _____
- _____
- _____

One

Beautiful

step at
a time

# 3 Words That Can Give Me Extra Confidence

DATE:

- _____
- _____
- _____

DATE:

- _____
- _____
- _____

DATE:

- _____
- _____
- _____

DATE:

- _____
- _____
- _____

DATE:

- _____
- _____
- _____

DATE:

- _____
- _____
- _____

DATE:

- _____
- _____
- _____

I can level up
my confidence

# 3 Beautiful Ways To Love Myself Today

DATE:
- _____
- _____
- _____

DATE:
- _____
- _____
- _____

DATE:
- _____
- _____
- _____

DATE:
- _____
- _____
- _____

DATE:
- _____
- _____
- _____

DATE:
- _____
- _____
- _____

DATE:
- _____
- _____
- _____

# 3 Things That Gives Me That Sparkling Feeling

DATE:

- _____
- _____
- _____

DATE:

- _____
- _____
- _____

DATE:

- _____
- _____
- _____

DATE:

- _____
- _____
- _____

DATE:

- _____
- _____
- _____

DATE:

- _____
- _____
- _____

DATE:

- _____
- _____
- _____

I just
decided to
sparkle
today.
That's it.

# 3 People Who Made Me Smile Today

DATE:

- _____
- _____
- _____

DATE:

- _____
- _____
- _____

DATE:

- _____
- _____
- _____

DATE:

- _____
- _____
- _____

DATE:

- _____
- _____
- _____

DATE:

- _____
- _____
- _____

DATE:

- _____
- _____
- _____

i stay
close to
people and
things that
makes me
happy

# 3 Words To Help Me Stay Positive

DATE:
- _____
- _____
- _____

DATE:
- _____
- _____
- _____

DATE:
- _____
- _____
- _____

DATE:
- _____
- _____
- _____

DATE:
- _____
- _____
- _____

DATE:
- _____
- _____
- _____

DATE:
- _____
- _____
- _____

Staying positive doesn't mean
you have to be happy all the time.
It means that even on hard days,
you know that better days
are coming.

# 3 Quick Ways I Can Look and Feel Fabulous

**DATE:**
- _____
- _____
- _____

**DATE:**
- _____
- _____
- _____

**DATE:**
- _____
- _____
- _____

**DATE:**
- _____
- _____
- _____

**DATE:**
- _____
- _____
- _____

**DATE:**
- _____
- _____
- _____

**DATE:**
- _____
- _____
- _____

Be *fabulous.*

# 3 Images of Myself That Gives Me So Much Courage

DATE:
- _____
- _____
- _____

DATE:
- _____
- _____
- _____

DATE:
- _____
- _____
- _____

DATE:
- _____
- _____
- _____

DATE:
- _____
- _____
- _____

DATE:
- _____
- _____
- _____

DATE:
- _____
- _____
- _____

I AM
FEARLESS

# 3 Priorities That Can Help Me Succeed

DATE:
- 
- 
- 

DATE:
- 
- 
- 

DATE:
- 
- 
- 

DATE:
- 
- 
- 

DATE:
- 
- 
- 

DATE:
- 
- 
- 

DATE:
- 
- 
-

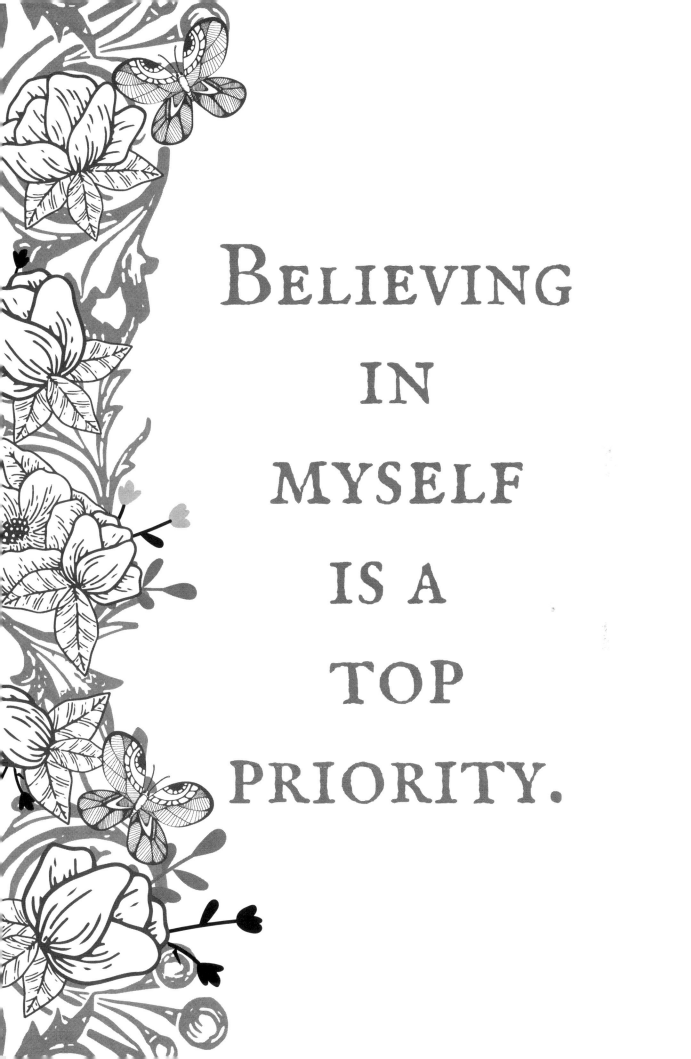

BELIEVING IN MYSELF IS A TOP PRIORITY.

# 3 Moments in My Life I Am Really Proud Of

DATE:
- _____
- _____
- _____

DATE:
- _____
- _____
- _____

DATE:
- _____
- _____
- _____

DATE:
- _____
- _____
- _____

DATE:
- _____
- _____
- _____

DATE:
- _____
- _____
- _____

DATE:
- _____
- _____
- _____

It doesn't matter what's been
written in my life so far...

It's how I fill up the rest
of the pages that counts.

# 3 Childhood Memories That Felt Magical

**DATE:**

- _____
- _____
- _____

**DATE:**

- _____
- _____
- _____

**DATE:**

- _____
- _____
- _____

**DATE:**

- _____
- _____
- _____

**DATE:**

- _____
- _____
- _____

**DATE:**

- _____
- _____
- _____

**DATE:**

- _____
- _____
- _____

I OPEN MY EYES TO
ALL THE WONDER
AROUND ME.

# 3 Ways I Can Be Happy Even When I'm Alone

DATE:
- _____
- _____
- _____

DATE:
- _____
- _____
- _____

DATE:
- _____
- _____
- _____

DATE:
- _____
- _____
- _____

DATE:
- _____
- _____
- _____

DATE:
- _____
- _____
- _____

DATE:
- _____
- _____
- _____

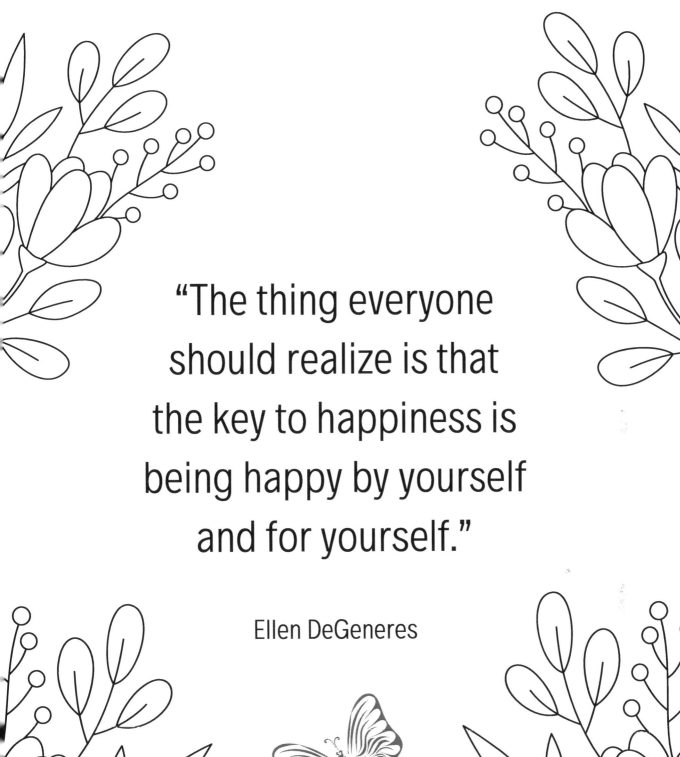

"The thing everyone should realize is that the key to happiness is being happy by yourself and for yourself."

Ellen DeGeneres

# 3 Things I Wish to Spend More Time On

DATE:
- 
- 
- 

DATE:
- 
- 
- 

DATE:
- 
- 
- 

DATE:
- 
- 
- 

DATE:
- 
- 
- 

DATE:
- 
- 
- 

DATE:
- 
- 
-

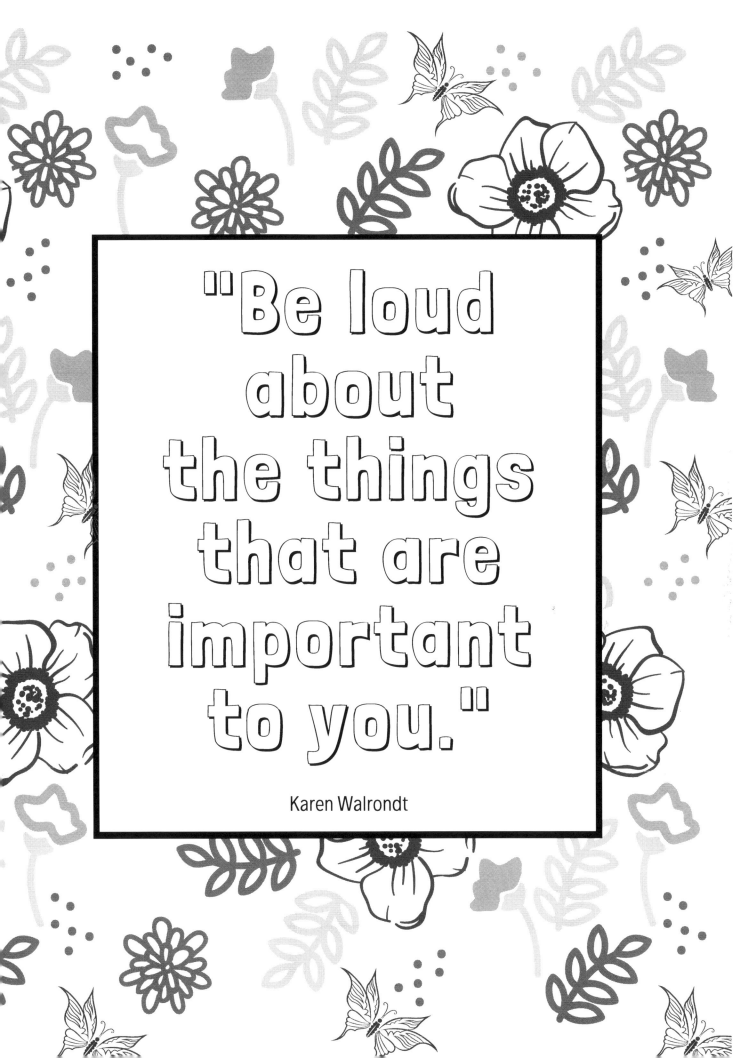

"Be loud about the things that are important to you."

Karen Walrondt

# 3 Miracles That I Am Always Thankful For

DATE:
- _____
- _____
- _____

DATE:
- _____
- _____
- _____

DATE:
- _____
- _____
- _____

DATE:
- _____
- _____
- _____

DATE:
- _____
- _____
- _____

DATE:
- _____
- _____
- _____

DATE:
- _____
- _____
- _____

Today is a miracle.

# 3 Greatest Achievements of My Life So Far

DATE:
- _____
- _____
- _____

DATE:
- _____
- _____
- _____

DATE:
- _____
- _____
- _____

DATE:
- _____
- _____
- _____

DATE:
- _____
- _____
- _____

DATE:
- _____
- _____
- _____

DATE:
- _____
- _____
- _____

my Wings
*already exist...*
ALL I HAVE
TO DO
is fly

# 3 Things I Am Most Grateful For Today

DATE:
- _____
- _____
- _____

DATE:
- _____
- _____
- _____

DATE:
- _____
- _____
- _____

DATE:
- _____
- _____
- _____

DATE:
- _____
- _____
- _____

DATE:
- _____
- _____
- _____

DATE:
- _____
- _____
- _____

# 3 Changes That Can Make Me Happier

DATE:
- _____
- _____
- _____

DATE:
- _____
- _____
- _____

DATE:
- _____
- _____
- _____

DATE:
- _____
- _____
- _____

DATE:
- _____
- _____
- _____

DATE:
- _____
- _____
- _____

DATE:
- _____
- _____
- _____

I HAVE THE POWER

TO CHANGE MY LIFE

# 3 Negative Feelings That I Must Let Go

DATE:
- _____
- _____
- _____

DATE:
- _____
- _____
- _____

DATE:
- _____
- _____
- _____

DATE:
- _____
- _____
- _____

DATE:
- _____
- _____
- _____

DATE:
- _____
- _____
- _____

DATE:
- _____
- _____
- _____

Feelings are
just visitors.
Let them come,
and let them go...

# 3 Lessons That Made Me Stronger Today

DATE:
- _____
- _____
- _____

DATE:
- _____
- _____
- _____

DATE:
- _____
- _____
- _____

DATE:
- _____
- _____
- _____

DATE:
- _____
- _____
- _____

DATE:
- _____
- _____
- _____

DATE:
- _____
- _____
- _____

The pain
I feel today
will be the
strength
I will feel
tomorrow.

# 3 Thoughts to Help Me Overcome Obstacles

**DATE:**

- _____
- _____
- _____

**DATE:**

- _____
- _____
- _____

**DATE:**

- _____
- _____
- _____

**DATE:**

- _____
- _____
- _____

**DATE:**

- _____
- _____
- _____

**DATE:**

- _____
- _____
- _____

**DATE:**

- _____
- _____
- _____

I Am Strong

# 3 Ways I Can Be an Answer to Somebody Else's Prayer

**DATE:**

- _____
- _____
- _____

**DATE:**

- _____
- _____
- _____

**DATE:**

- _____
- _____
- _____

**DATE:**

- _____
- _____
- _____

**DATE:**

- _____
- _____
- _____

**DATE:**

- _____
- _____
- _____

**DATE:**

- _____
- _____
- _____

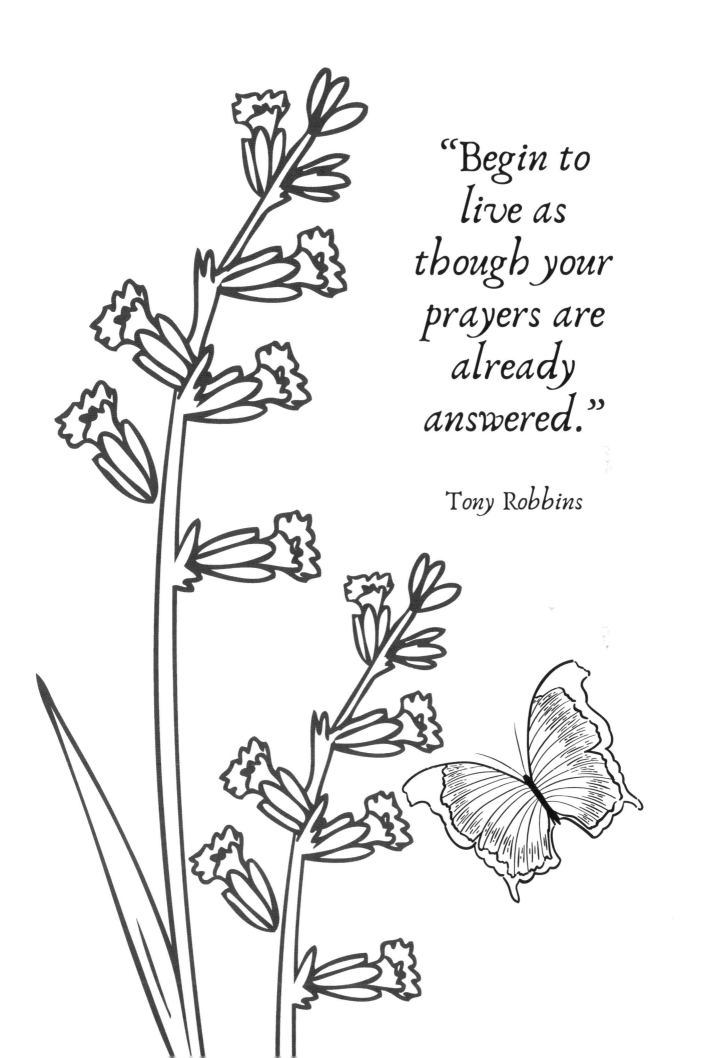

"Begin to live as though your prayers are already answered."

Tony Robbins

# 3 Positive Things I Wish to Happen in the Future

DATE:
- _____
- _____
- _____

DATE:
- _____
- _____
- _____

DATE:
- _____
- _____
- _____

DATE:
- _____
- _____
- _____

DATE:
- _____
- _____
- _____

DATE:
- _____
- _____
- _____

DATE:
- _____
- _____
- _____

*"Always believe that something wonderful is about to happen."*
~ S. S. Dhillon

# 3 Traits That Makes Me Extra Unique

DATE:
- _____
- _____
- _____

DATE:
- _____
- _____
- _____

DATE:
- _____
- _____
- _____

DATE:
- _____
- _____
- _____

DATE:
- _____
- _____
- _____

DATE:
- _____
- _____
- _____

DATE:
- _____
- _____
- _____

# 3 Things I Want to Say To My Future Self

DATE:
- 
- 
- 

DATE:
- 
- 
- 

DATE:
- 
- 
- 

DATE:
- 
- 
- 

DATE:
- 
- 
- 

DATE:
- 
- 
- 

DATE:
- 
- 
-

The past is in my head. The future is in my hands.

# 3 Actions That Can Lead Me Closer to My Goals

DATE:

- _____
- _____
- _____

DATE:

- _____
- _____
- _____

DATE:

- _____
- _____
- _____

DATE:

- _____
- _____
- _____

DATE:

- _____
- _____
- _____

DATE:

- _____
- _____
- _____

DATE:

- _____
- _____
- _____

I am a Masterpiece in Progress

# 3 Priceless Gifts I Want to Give to Myself

**DATE:**
- _____
- _____
- _____

**DATE:**
- _____
- _____
- _____

**DATE:**
- _____
- _____
- _____

**DATE:**
- _____
- _____
- _____

**DATE:**
- _____
- _____
- _____

**DATE:**
- _____
- _____
- _____

**DATE:**
- _____
- _____
- _____

# being happy is the greatest gift I can give to myself

# 3 Things That Inspires Me to Do the Impossible

**DATE:**
- _____
- _____
- _____

**DATE:**
- _____
- _____
- _____

**DATE:**
- _____
- _____
- _____

**DATE:**
- _____
- _____
- _____

**DATE:**
- _____
- _____
- _____

**DATE:**
- _____
- _____
- _____

**DATE:**
- _____
- _____
- _____

"*You must find the place inside yourself where nothing is impossible.*"

Deepak Chopra

# 3 Happy Memories I Want to Keep Forever

DATE:
- _____
- _____
- _____

DATE:
- _____
- _____
- _____

DATE:
- _____
- _____
- _____

DATE:
- _____
- _____
- _____

DATE:
- _____
- _____
- _____

DATE:
- _____
- _____
- _____

DATE:
- _____
- _____
- _____

 # COLOR TEST PAGE

dear self,

 i love you... from now on, i promise you that you will always have my heart.

 and no matter how tough life gets, or how heavy the burden i've been given, i am steady in the knowledge that I can always find the way back to you.

 on days when i feel the need for a confidence boost, i can easily pick up this book, read the powerful words inside, and write more powerful words of my own!

 and on days when i just want to relax and let my mind focus on calming colors and beauty of nature, i can simply paint my creative magic on these pages and allow all doubts and fears completely melt away...

 love,

 _____

Hope you enjoyed this book. We wish it made you smile
and made you feel stronger on days when you need it.

If you have questions or just want to share your thoughts, you can email
us at **simplepsychologypress@gmail.com.**

Also, feel free to leave us a review on **Amazon.com** to help us learn more
about your creative journey. Cheers!

Printed in Great Britain
by Amazon